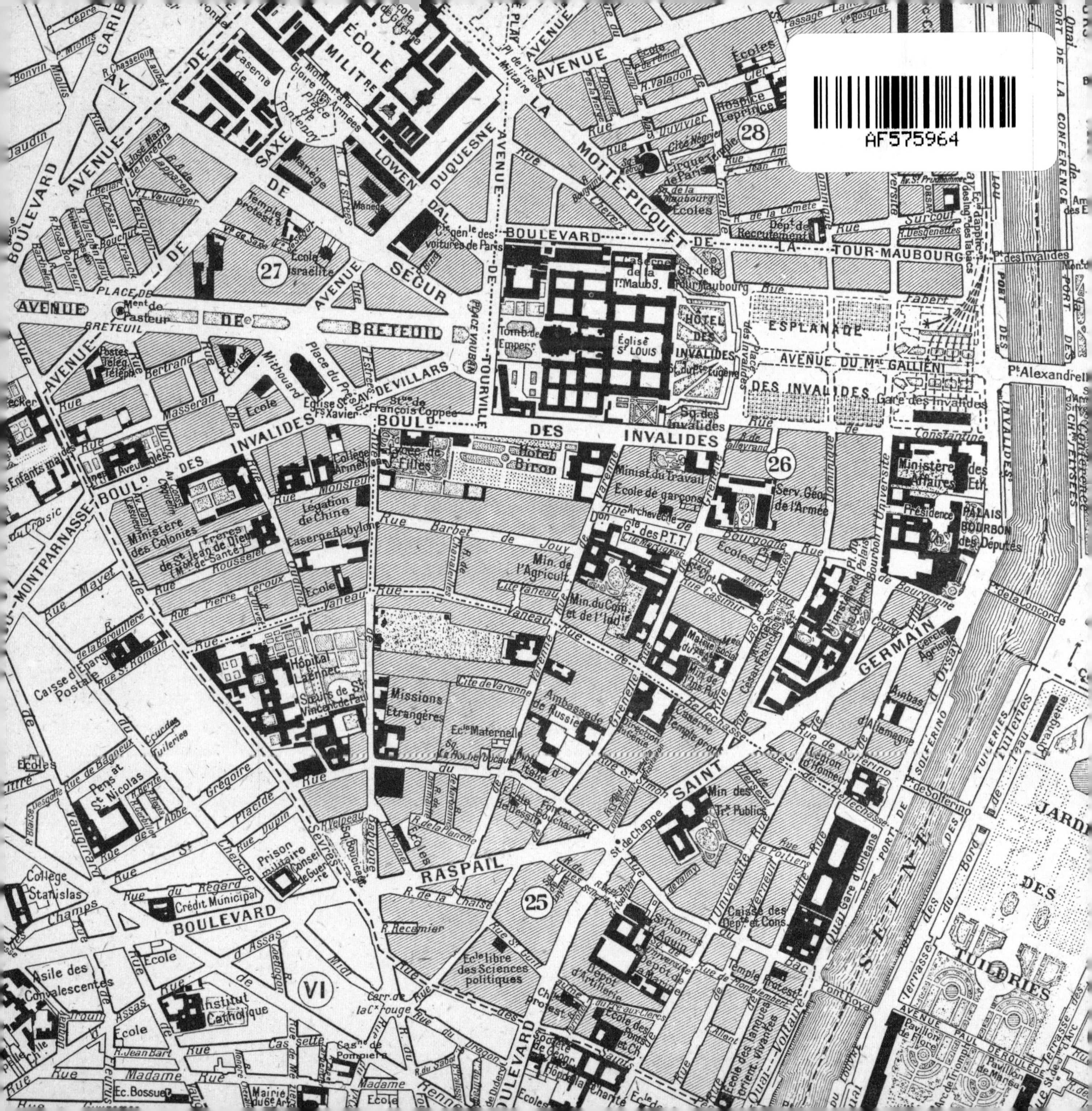

AF575964
ÉCOLE MILITAIRE
Caserne de Fontenoy
Monument à la Gloire des Armées
Place de Fontenoy
AVENUE DE SAXE
AVENUE DE LOWENDAL
AVENUE DUQUESNE
AVENUE DE LA MOTTE-PICQUET
BOULEVARD DE LA TOUR-MAUBOURG
AVENUE DE SÉGUR
AVENUE DE BRETEUIL
PLACE DE BRETEUIL
Mᵗ de Pasteur
Temple protest.
École israélite
27
28
26
25
VI
Manège
Cᶦᵉ génˡᵉ des voitures de Paris
Caserne de la Tʳ Maubᵍ
Sq. de la Tour Maubourg
HÔTEL DES INVALIDES
Tomb. de l'Empereur
Église Sᵗ LOUIS
PLACE VAUBAN
AVENUE DE TOURVILLE
ESPLANADE DES INVALIDES
AVENUE DU Mᵃˡ GALLIENI
Gare des Invalides
Pᵗ des Invalides
Pᵗ Alexandre III
Rue Fabert
Rue de Constantine
Sq. des Invalides
Église Sᵗ Fˢ Xavier
AV. DE VILLARS
Place du Présᵗ Mithouard
Sᵗᵉ de François Coppée
BOULᴰ DES INVALIDES
BOULᴰ MONTPARNASSE
Hôtel Biron
Lycée de Jⁿᵉˢ Filles
Ministère des Colonies
Frères de Sᵗ Jean de Dieu
Légation de Chine
Caserne Babylone
Rue Barbet de Jouy
Min. de l'Agricult.
Ministᵉ du Travail
École de garçons
Archevêché
Gᵗᵉ des P.T.T.
Serv. Géoᵍ de l'Armée
Ministère des Affaires Étr.
Présidence
PALAIS BOURBON
Chᵇʳᵉ des Députés
Pᵗ de la Concorde
PORT DE LA CONFÉRENCE
PORT DES CHAMPS ÉLYSÉES
Min. du Comᶜᵉ et de l'Indᵗʳⁱᵉ
Rue de Varenne
Rue de Grenelle
Rue de Bourgogne
Rue Vaneau
Hôpital Laënnec
Sœurs de Sᵗ Vincent de Paul
Missions Étrangères
Ambassade de Russie
Écᵒˡᵉ Maternelle
Cité de Varenne
BOULEVARD SAINT GERMAIN
Cercle Agricole
Ambasᵈᵉ d'Allemagne
Légion d'Honneur
Rue de Solférino
Pᵗ de Solférino
Min. des Trˣ Publics
Caserne Temple protᵗ
Rue de Bellechasse
Rue de Babylone
Rue de Sèvres
Caisse d'Épargne Postale
Pensᵃᵗ Sᵗ Nicolas
Rue de l'Abbé Grégoire
Prison militaire
Conseil de Guerre
BOULEVARD RASPAIL
Rue du Regard
Crédit Municipal
Collège Stanislas
Rue Notre-Dame des Champs
R. Récamier
R. de la Chaise
Écᵒˡᵉ libre des Sciences politiques
Sᵗ Thomas d'Aquin
Dépôt d'Artillerie
Caisse des Dépᵗˢ et Cons.
Gare d'Orléans
Quai d'Orsay
SEINE
TERRASSE DU BORD DE L'EAU
JARDIN DES TUILERIES
Orangerie
AVENUE PAUL DÉROULÈDE
Pavillon de Flore
Pavillon de Marsan
Pont Royal
Temple protestᵗ
École des Ponts et Ch.
École des langues orient. vivantes
Quai Voltaire
Asile des Convalescentes
Institut Catholique
Rue d'Assas
Rue de Vaugirard
Rue Madame
Rue Cassette
Casⁿᵉ de Pompiers
Carr. de la Cˣ rouge
Rue du Dragon
Ec. Bossuet
Mairie du 6ᵉ Arᵗ
Hôpital de la Charité
BOULEVARD

Arrondissements

Daryl Hine

Arrondissements

The Porcupine's Quill, Inc.

For A B

T'introduire dans mon histoire ...

No mere tour de force, like so many of my productions, though rhymed and metred to a fare-thee-well, this, my *Desiderium Lutetiae* (or Nostalgie de la Boue) is all that remains of a much longer but less excursive prose memoir, thank goodness unpublished, entitled *A Still Salt Pool.* There, with queer but not quite queer enough aesthetic results, I altered not only my person but my sex, in the manner of Henry James. More impersonal but hardly asexual, the present dizzy and I hope dizzying verse sucks up, with all the omnivorousness of a vacuum, the detritus of Paris by day and night, the not very naughty and scarcely gay capital where I did my first and most arduous graduate work, in what at the time looked like life. Of all the names of the dear and deplorable living and dead that might have been dropped here, none is cited, with the partial pseudonymic exception of Folly, the presiding deity of those years between 1958 and 1962, years that always seem in retrospect so much longer than they were at the time, when they simply seemed a lifetime. In the place of David and Joe and Philippe and John and Patrick and Sandy, just for starters, whirl the districts or *arrondissements* of Paris, those Dantesque circles in three of which (the third, sixth and seventh) I dwelt, while visiting and occasionally hanging out in others. An indefatigable and indigent pedestrian, there was a spring in my step in those days. Now the footfall of Autumn dogs my heels, while to my case-hardened ear these impetuous stanzas do not walk, they run. It is no accident that *souvenir* has had to be imported into our language, as a memento that we have nothing in English more fragrant than 'reminder', with its discouraging echo of 'remainder', themselves both Latin memories, unless it be the rather rueful *agenbite of inwit.* I wrote the following lines over a decade ago. A tale like that implicit here is encoded in no one night, no, nor in a thousand and one mornings. Borrowings or outright pillage from various French poets will be too obvious to those more familiar than I with the Bibliothèque Nationale. Yet the only real and best reason for the re-edition of *Arrondissements* seems to me the pictures – each worth a thousand words – furnished by my fellow sojourners in the City of Light. Of these the poet and pornographer John Glassco would most approve of such 'Pale skin books with red-faced prefaces.'

Daryl Hine
Evanston, 1988

Ier *Palais Royal*

A foreign city in a foreign language:
Errors you will find your way around
Less by misconstruction of an image
Idiomatic as the underground
Than by reference to the lost and found
Out-of-date semantic luggage
And archaic sentimental slang which
Used to mean so much. Beware of the sound,
Volumes of experience rebound,
Sense can take care of itself. Abandoned baggage,
I sought to celebrate you, not confound;
Apart from the smarts you brought me, *grand dommage,*
A throne's stowaway, you still astound
The razor's edge dividing youth from age.

Paris '87
E Bailey

IIe *Bibliothèque Nationale*

'Nothing but a pack of cards' obscurely comments
Dimbulb, whose enlightenment must prove
A catalogue of incandescent moments –
Years shrunk to days, hours hung like months –
That categorically survive
Oblivion in a cross-indexed grave
With other mortal meantimes, to achieve
The brazen afterlife of monuments.
This mental midden, almost as immense
As the world it was the wonder of,
Which it can't comprehend but complements,
Does it explain what evidence we have,
An ennui ingenuity augments,
Cruising the pages of the treasure-trove?

CANCALE
AU ROCHE
DES HALLES

IIIe *Arts et Métiers*

There are shady purlieus no one wanders
Except in speculation, ways
Affected by perpetual pretenders,
Amateur meanders that amaze
The tourist who professionally blunders
Into labyrinths through which no stranger strays
Prepared. What lies or (literally) lays
Behind the glazed pentameters of windows
With their drawn, blind, introspective gaze,
The passer-by pedestrianly wonders,
Besides florid wallpaper and bidets?
The encyclopaedic street surrenders
Secrets sometimes lost in paraphrase:
Moods, tenses, persons, numbers, genders.

IVe *Quai d'Anjou*

Superficially the envelope
Sports the legend, *Addressee Unknown:*
The familiar, arbitrary shape
Of the letters seems strange at the same
Time you recognize them as your own,
Returned to Sender. Stereotype,
Signature or pseudonym,
The ultimate enigma is your name.
Too trivial for the microscope,
Repetitious as the gramophone,
The recycled syllables escape
The statement you were brash enough to sign
Forever yours, the sort of tripe
One writes when one is twenty-one.

Ve *Quartier Latin*

Jardin des Plaintes, Pandémonium, Coup de Grâce:
Starred sites we circled all night long,
Apart from a crepuscular embrace
Incommunicado. Being young,
With other clubs invited to belong
To, nationality, gender, class,
Impressed us then as a disgrace,
Almost an unconscionable wrong,
To which, not quite unconsciously, we clung
As if for life, in spite, or just in case,
Like friendship, unexpected as a song
Before sunrise in a silent place,
Or the comforts of our mother tongue
Overheard on some café *terrasse.*

VIe *Institut Français*

Six flights below my balcony the traffic
Percolates the narrow rue de Seine,
At the same time tepid and terrific,
Uninteresting and obscene.
The footstep on the stair of a petrific
Visitor unnaturally soon
Arrests the contemplation of specific
Images that persecute the sane.
Again today deciphers pornographic
Night's incomprehensible design,
Every superstitious hieroglyphic
Reified by an explicit sun,
Shades uncensored by the soporific
Darkness of which dreams are partisan.

VIIe *Chambre des Députés*

Overshadowed by the Ministry of War,
We shared an absurdly furnished flat,
Dubious *Empire* and *Directoire,*
With an early modern bathroom, that
Winter, until the tasteless coup d'état
Of Spring, insurgent in silk underwear.
Folly, female, fortyish and fat,
Found me a companionable if queer
Cohabitant of her cosy habitat,
A ménage of inconvenience where
We lived like dog and wife and man and cat,
Compatible antagonists aware
Of a temporary tit-for-tat,
Like it was, or rather, as it were.

VIIIe *Elysée*

Anatomy of a mistake,
The structure of affairs is uniform,
Part of the pathological mystique
To which romantic accidents conform.
Infatuation's formidable physique
And infant physiognomy confirm
The pattern of attraction, one unique
To fantasy's Elysium.
Thus enfranchised of that funny farm,
Unfortunate affection seems a freak
Of feeling, the inevitable form
That fatal fascination has to take.
How often out of nightmare do we wake
Beside the one whom we were fleeing from?

IXe *Opéra*

Tedious the intervals of living
Between the acts, etc.,
Clichés as distinct from moving
Parts depicted by the camera,
Interludes in an indulgent era
Dissipated by the disapproving
Scrutiny of tomorrow
Which will, I fear, be unforgiving;
Then delinquent evening arriving
Splendid in her twinkling tiara,
An hour late, delayed by daylight saving,
A dusky demi-mondaine with an aura
Of the Belle Epoque, surviving
As a backdrop to the opera.

Xe *Gare du Nord*

Haunted by arrivals and departures,
The desperate farewell of handkerchiefs,
This dingy greenhouse architecture nurtures
An exotic growth of greetings, griefs
And brief encounters under iron arches
Overlooked by smutty petroglyphs.
Having said goodbye to make-beliefs
And all a single backward glance can purchase,
Through the unsympathetic crowd one searches
Among reunions, tears and tiffs
Unfamiliarity that tortures
The traveller with interminable ifs
For those extraordinary features
Familiarity enfeoffs.

XIe *Saint Ambroise*

Never underestimate the slogans
Scribbled overnight in public places –
Ambrose Go Home! Power to the Pagans –
Nor the civilization that defaces
These legends fabulous as dragons,
Pale skin books with red-faced prefaces,
Profane initials, sacred organs
Erased to make way for an oasis
Paradise of perfect paragons
Whose nomenclature graphically embraces
Dead ends and picturesque parentheses,
Ruinous beginnings that seemed bargains
Once, the revolutionary faces
Of those who let bygones be bygones.

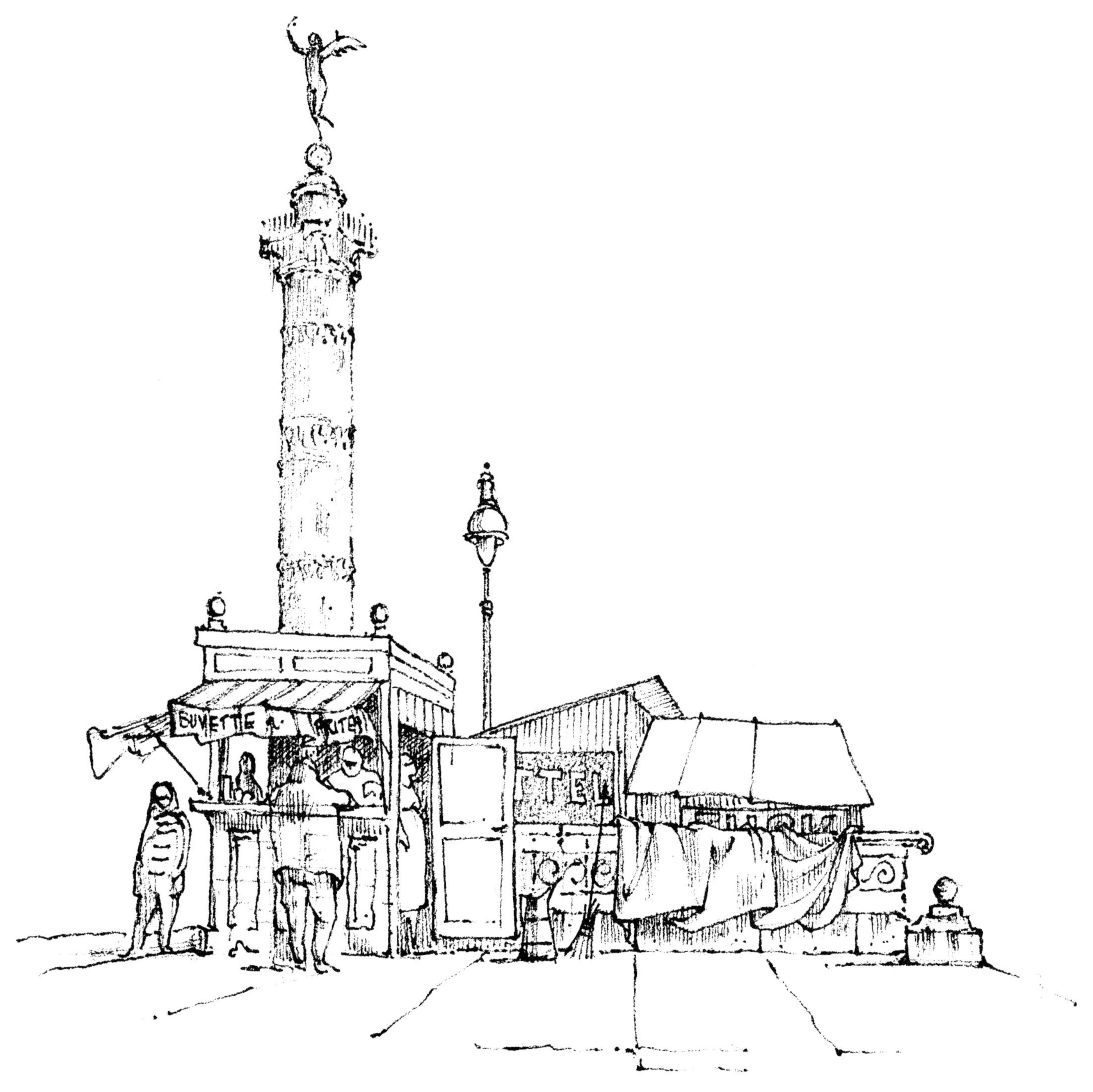
BUVETTE

XII[e] *Porte de Vincennes*

Irradiating like a dull penumbra
The suburbs of the citadel of light,
Detours without character or number
Advertise contemporary blight;
Here history, inimical to slumber,
Held up the royal nincompoop in flight
Just because she could not disencumber
Herself of her ancestral appetite.
The autumn of *le feu régime,* remember?
The eve of what we came to call The Fright,
The first Brumaire – is that November? –
Alias All Hallows' Night,
With the Sun King an extinguished ember,
And evergreens in periwigs of white.

BAR

XIIIe *Salpetrière*

The thirteenth returns – yet it is the first
Time we proximately failed to meet
Across the gap our ages made reversed,
That post meridian I watched you beat
Time at your open window, indiscreet
As innocence incongruously cursed
With a precocious portion of man's meat.
In solitary vice immensely versed,
I kept time while puberty rehearsed
The age-old ritual of self-defeat,
Pricking the tumescent bubble till it burst,
An agon adolescence can repeat
Ad nauseam, while sympathy, in heat,
Next door to the fountain dies of thirst.

XIVe *Observatoire*

Obvious from the Observatory,
After the abdication of the moon
Heaven explicates a bedtime story
Full of incident and interest, humane
Like anything significant to man,
The everlasting, transitory
Celestial phenomenon
In all its superannuated glory,
A *roman fleuve* that one is always sorry
To see abridged by dawn. The stars remain
Secure in their orbits, never in a hurry,
Worlds superior to yours and mine,
Dispassionate, explanatory,
Suggesting more than they can ever mean.

XVe *Vaugirard*

Tabula rasa, fair and vacant page,
Impenetrable open book unlined
By the ineradicable afterthoughts of age,
Inane impressions that outrage
The paper void its blankness can't defend,
What an idea, to be defined
According to the petty average
And calculated meanness of mankind,
Catalogued, confined
Captive in the cage,
Cosily conventional, of kind,
A jejune personage
Whose very emptiness may yet engage
The spirit when the flesh is out of mind.

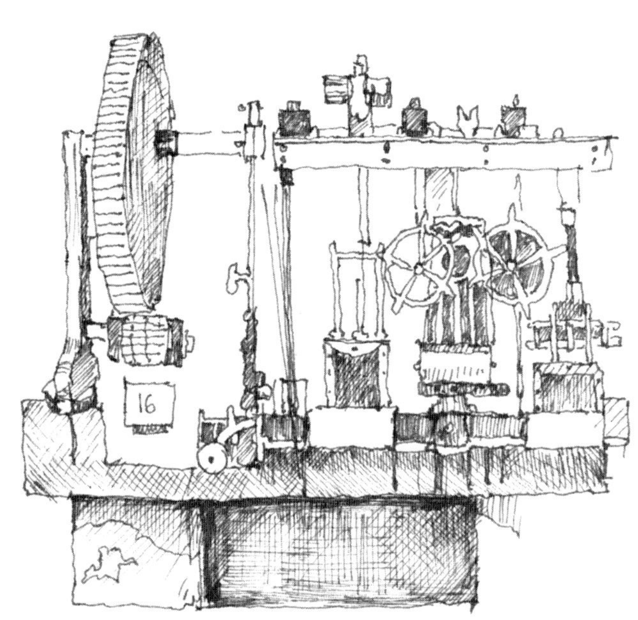
16

XVI[e] *Muette*

In eccentric circles memory
Like a longplaying record crazily revolves
Until the trivial, terminal melody
Abrupts, its lifelong dissonance dissolves
Into the operative gears and valves
Of time's Edwardian machinery.
Song concocts some problems that it solves
Often with an astonished Q.E.D.,
A rational equation that involves
Real variables, you and me,
Coefficient and unequal halves,
Imaginary numerals, a to b,
The co-ordinate conjunction of our selves
Or the cyphers that we used to be.

XVII[e] *Ternes*

Absence is a type of convalescence.
Committed to this gothic hospital
Where life has been protracted to a sentence
Episodic, periodical
As a phantom cast upon a wall,
Grotesque, distorted, menacing, immense
Out of all proportion to the small
Object that caused it, I begin to sense
The possibility of being well,
Eventual recuperation from a spell
Baneful mainly in the present tense.
Practising your absence as a penance,
Like an ascetic anticipating hell,
I come to appreciate the presence
Of the sacrament that says it all.

XVIIIe *Montmartre*

Kindness is for mortals, only they,
In this world reluctantly at home,
Find it an amazing place to stay,
Sympathetic as a rented room
Where one is here tomorrow, gone today,
Just the sort of customer for whom
Love is something to be thrown away
Eventually, like a broken comb.
Running backwards as a palindrome,
Time will be deciphered anyway,
Though the implications of that poem
Originally resist a résumé.
Under the superstructure of the dome
The phone is dumb that had so much to say.

XIXe *Amérique, Combat*

Token of that humorous umpteenth
Memorable day misspent in bed,
A singular combat celebrated since
By incessant reruns in my head
At whose indecent vividness I wince,
All the evidence I loved you once
Recollected, everything you said
Elected as a god upon a plinth,
Take this text which you have never read
And never may, perhaps, erotic prints
Indelible as life itself whose length
Is measured in catastrophes instead
Of strophes, revised ineptly to the *n*th
Degree. Before you read me, we'll be dead.

XXe *Père Lachaise*

Death's exclusive suburb, where the doors
Open upon empty anterooms,
Welcomes a few tardy visitors
Cryptically on mortal afternoons.
The bogus nineteenth century adores,
Albeit in fantastic undertones,
What our sophisticated taste deplores,
Dramatic last words and attractive glooms.
Among marshals, musicians, courtesans and bores
Ranked according to profession, who presumes
To flout society's posthumous laws?
Statuettesque among the stolid tombs
Above our witty saint's dishonoured bones
Oscar's ithyphallic angel soars.

JOE PLASKETT met Daryl Hine when the poet, only fifteen at the time, attended one of his exhibitions in British Columbia. Several years later, when Hine arrived in Paris, Plaskett welcomed him and introduced him to his circle of friends. (Cover illustrations, frontispiece, Poem XIV.)

DAVID HILL, Joe Plaskett and Daryl Hine were frequently together in Paris during the late 'fifties. The poet sat for portraits by both artists. (Poems I and VIII.)

VIRGIL BURNETT met Daryl Hine when Joe Plaskett brought the poet aboard the *Inge,* a yacht anchored in the Seine at the Pont de l'Alma, on which Burnett lived in 1957. (Poems VI, IX, XII, XVIII, the jacket portrait of the poet and the caricature facing this page.)

ELIZABETH BAILEY has been a frequent visitor to the house in the Marais where Joe Plaskett and David Hill had studios, and which Plaskett still occupies when he is in France. (Poems II, III, VII, and XI.)

ISABELLA STEFANESCU sketched in most of the arrondissements of Paris during the summer of 1987. (Poems IV, V, X, XIII, XV, XVI, XVII, XIX, and XX.)

CATALOGUING IN PUBLICATION DATA

Hine, Daryl, 1936-
Arrondissements

Poems.
Edited by Virgil Burnett.
ISBN 0-88984-130-6

I. Burnett, Virgil. II. Title.

PS8515.I56A87 1988 C811'.54 C88-095141-9
PR9199.3.H56A87 1988

Originally published as part of a collection of poems called *Daylight Saving* © 1975 by Daryl Hine. Reprinted by arrangement with Atheneum Publishers, an imprint of Macmillan Publishing Company. This edition is published by The Porcupine's Quill, Inc., 68 Main Street, Erin, Ontario NOB 1TO with the financial assistance of the Canada Council and the Ontario Arts Council.

Distributed by The University of Toronto Press, 5201 Dufferin Street, Downsview, Ontario. Printed and bound in January, 1989 by The Porcupine's Quill. The stock is Baskerville, and the type, Ehrhardt.

VII
22
23
PALAIS DU LUXEMBOURG
JARDIN DU LUXEMBOURG
SAINT GERMAIN
MONTPARNASSE
BOULEVARD
RASPAIL
École des Sciences politiques
École de Dessin
Missions Étrangères
Square Boucicaut
Conseil de Guerre Prison militaire
Hôpital Laënnec
Caisse d'Epargne Postale
Collège Stanislas
Lycée Montaigne
Dames Augustines de Ste Marie
Ec. Alsacne
Odéon
Musée
Petit Luxembourg
Sénat
Asile de Vieillards
Mairie du 6me Art.
PLACE St SULPICE
Soc. de Géographie
Dépôt d'Artillerie
Ec. des Mines
Marché
Écoles